Basketball Basics

Written by Kerrie Shanahan

Flying Start
to Literacy®

Contents

Introduction

All over the world, people play basketball.
It is a great way to have fun and stay fit.
Anyone can play – all you need is to know
the rules and have a go.

This book tells you how to get started.
It tells you what you will need and
how to play basketball.

What you need to play
A basketball

A basketball is a very bouncy ball. Basketballs come in different sizes for different age groups.

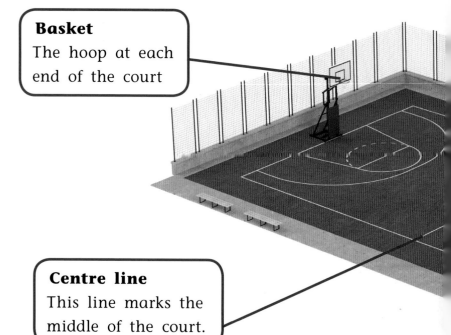

Basket
The hoop at each end of the court

Centre line
This line marks the middle of the court.

A basketball court

Basketball is played on a court. At each end of the court there is a goal, which has a backboard and a hoop.

There are lines on the court around each goal and a line across the centre of the court.

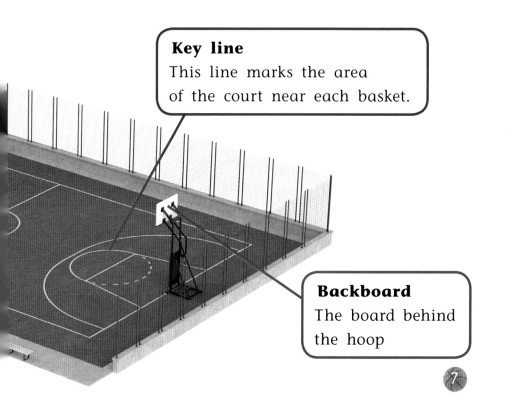

Key line
This line marks the area of the court near each basket.

Backboard
The board behind the hoop

Two teams

Basketball is played with two teams. Each team has between five and 10 players. Only five players from each team are on the court at the one time.

The players in a team can take turns being on the court. When one player is taken off the court and another player takes their place, this player is called a substitute.

Each player wears their team's uniform and has a number.

A referee

When two teams play a game of basketball, there is a person in charge who makes sure that both teams obey the rules. This person is called a referee.

How to play

Time

A game of basketball goes for about 40 minutes. A game has either two halves or four quarters. There is a break in-between each half or quarter.

Rules

The referee uses a whistle to start and stop the game. If a player on one team breaks a rule, the referee gives the ball to a player on the other team and they get a free pass.

The players on each team try to stop the players on the other team from passing or shooting the ball. If a player hits, pushes or slaps a player on the other team while trying to stop the ball, it is called a foul. The referee decides – he makes the call.

If a player gets five fouls, they must leave the court. They cannot come back on for the rest of the game.

Scoring

Each team tries to score points by throwing the basketball through the hoop at their end of the court. Every player is allowed to shoot goals.

To score, the ball can bounce off the backboard and through the hoop or just go straight through the hoop.

After one team shoots a basket, the other team gets to pass the ball in from the back of the court to restart the game.

If the ball misses the hoop, all the players can try to grab it. This is called a rebound.

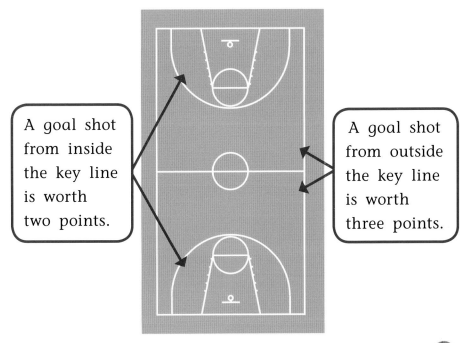

A goal shot from inside the key line is worth two points.

A goal shot from outside the key line is worth three points.

Basketball skills
How to shoot

Players who have a good shooting technique are better at scoring points.

1. Put one hand under the ball, with your wrist bent back.

2. Put your other hand on the side of the ball to balance it as your arm pushes the ball up into the air.

3. As the ball is released, flick the ball towards the hoop.

Moving the ball

Players can move the ball down the court towards their hoop in two ways.

Dribbling

The first way to move the ball down the court is by bouncing it with one hand as you run down the court. This is called dribbling.

Players can dribble for as long as they like. Once they stop and hold the ball in two hands, they are not allowed to start dribbling again. They have to pass the ball to another player.

Throwing and passing

The second way to move the ball down the court is by throwing or passing from one player to another. This is a fast way of moving the ball.

When a team has the ball, the players in that team spread out. If all the players are too close together, it is harder to pass or dribble the ball.

Defending

When one team has the ball, the other team needs to defend. This means making things difficult for the team with the ball to move and score.

The team that is defending tries to stay between the player with the ball and the basket. They can put their hands up high to make it difficult for the player with the ball to dribble, pass or shoot the ball.

Conclusion

Basketball is a fast-moving, high-scoring game. It is full of action with speedy play and energetic moves. Both boys and girls can play.

The best thing about basketball is that it is lots of fun and a great way to spend time with your friends.

Glossary

basket The hoop at each end of the court is called a basket.

defend Each team tries to stop the other team from passing or shooting the ball. This is called defending.

dribble To bounce the ball with one hand while running.

foul When one player unfairly contacts another player, it is called a foul.

rebound When the ball hits the hoop or the backboard and falls back into play, the player who catches the ball is said to have taken a rebound.

substitute A substitute is a player who replaces another player on the basketball court.